# Battered Lawyers

# Simon Bond

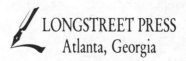 LONGSTREET PRESS
Atlanta, Georgia

and

INTERNATIONAL ART EXPRESSIONS INC.

Published by
LONGSTREET PRESS, INC. and INTERNATIONAL ART EXPRESSIONS INC.
2150 Newmarket Parkway
Suite 102
Marietta, Georgia 30067

Introduction copyright © 1990 by Daniel R. White
Illustrations copyright © 1990 by Simon Bond

Printed in the United States of America

1st printing, 1990

Library of Congress Catalog Number 90-061850

ISBN 0-929264-78-9

This book was printed by R. R. Donnelley & Sons, Harrisonburg, Virginia.
The text was set in Helvetica by Typo-Repro Service, Inc., Atlanta, Georgia.
Cover design by Mary Rowe, Lawrenceville, Georgia.

# Introduction

It is perhaps an indication of society's warm and enduring regard for the legal profession that so many people find mirth and merriment in jokes about lawyers. We feel free to smile at the law's foibles, secure in the knowledge that its pinstriped practitioners are not only confident enough to withstand the jest, but big-hearted and selfless enough to appreciate it.

Alternatively, of course, all those jokes may indicate a widespread urge to vomit on lawyers.

Who can say for sure?

In any event, lawyer lampooning is greeted these days with the approval and approbation of people from all walks of life — not only the rich and powerful, but who cares about the rest. Hence the virtual certainty that this wry volume will ultimately reside in the elite halls of best-sellerdom.

Simon ("His word is his") Bond is probably best known for his previous best seller (at 1.75 *million* copies and growing), *101 Uses for a Dead Cat*, an extensively researched and heavily documented look at one of the critical waste disposal problems confronting contemporary society. That Mr. Bond did not title the present book *101 Uses for a Dead Lawyer* is perhaps a reflection of his magnanimity of spirit, which the rest of us would do well to emulate.

Alternatively, of course, it may reflect the more intractable waste disposal problems posed by heavy use of attorneys.

Again, who can say for sure?

Either way, the fact is that this book needs no introduction. It has one because its subject is lawyers, which means a page or two of gratuitous verbiage conveys a sense of realism. I would also like to use it to say that if anybody knows what happened to the hubcaps on my '82 Volkswagen Rabbit, I would greatly appreciate getting them back — no questions asked.

Daniel R. White

Daniel R. White — attorney, humorist, celebrated convention speaker — wrote *The Official Lawyer's Handbook*, a national best-selling satire, as well as *White's Law Dictionary* and *What Lawyers Do*. His most recent work is *Trials and Tribulations — An Anthology of Appealing Legal Humor* (Catbird Press). He lives and practices in Washington, D.C.

3

"And I sentence you to four years imprisonment, plus two more years for the suit."

# ABRAHAM LINCOLN SENDS HIS FIRST BILL

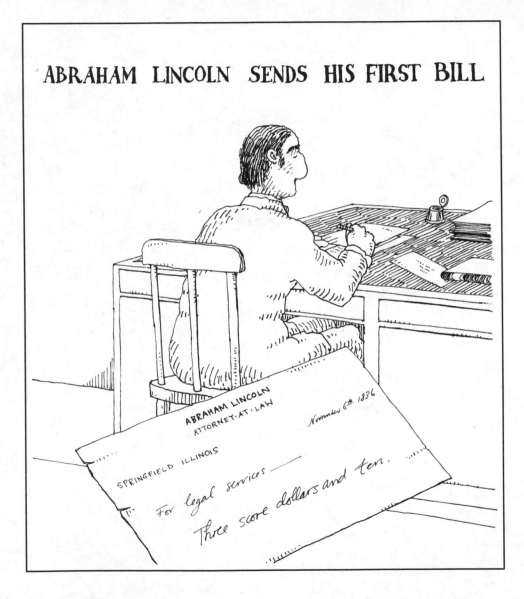

"Miss Frobisher, could you get me the State of Arizona versus the Apache Nation file?"

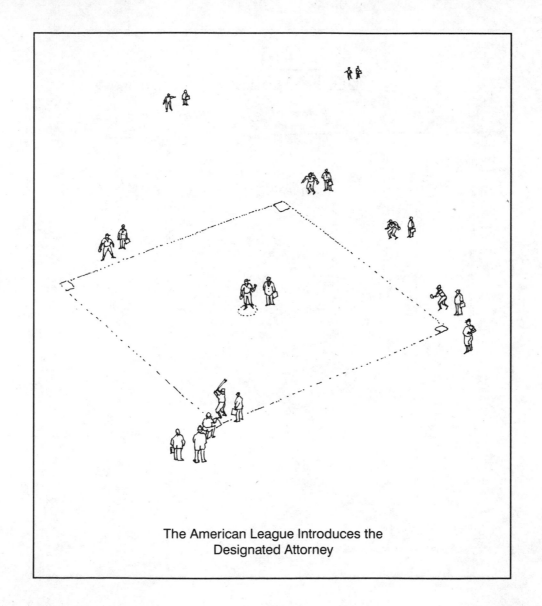

The American League Introduces the
Designated Attorney

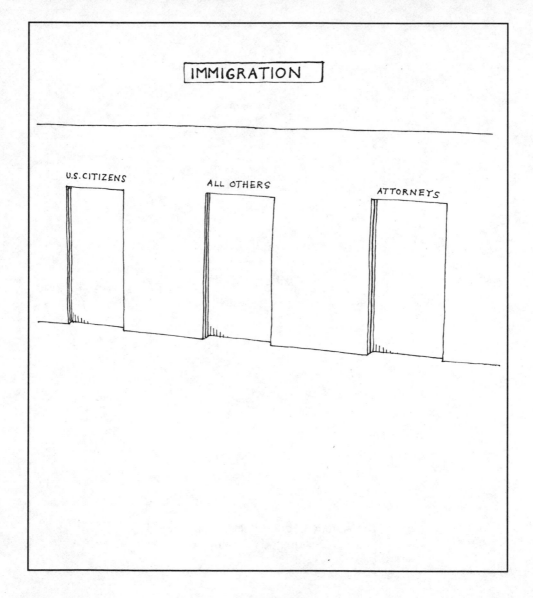

BRENDAN BULLDOCK
Attorney General

# THE RIGGED JURY

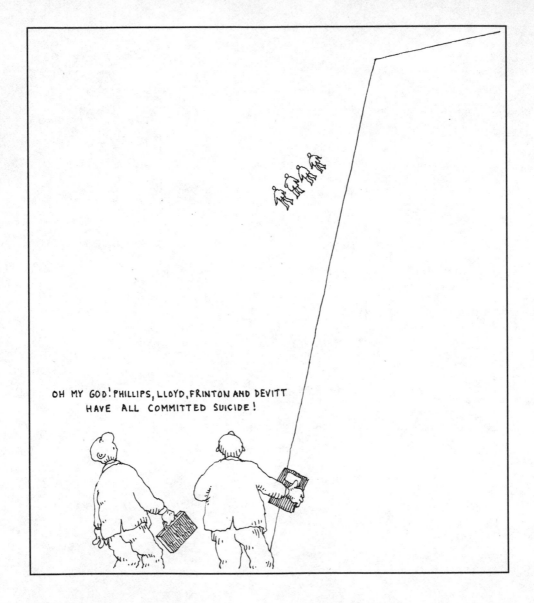

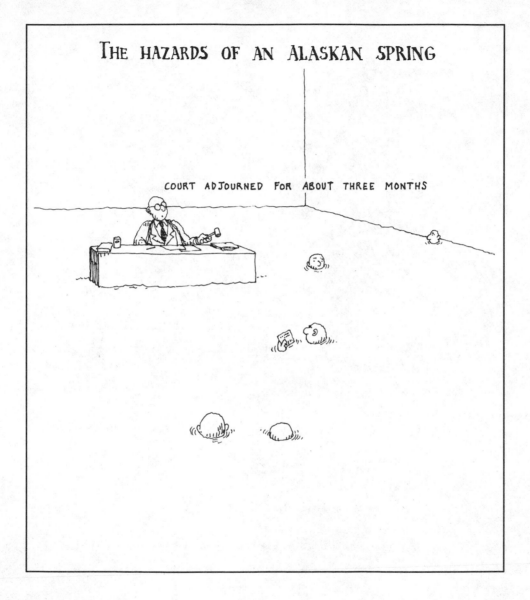

THESE MEN ARE LAWYERS...BUT I'M NOT SURE I'D RECOMMEND YOU USE ANY OF THEM.

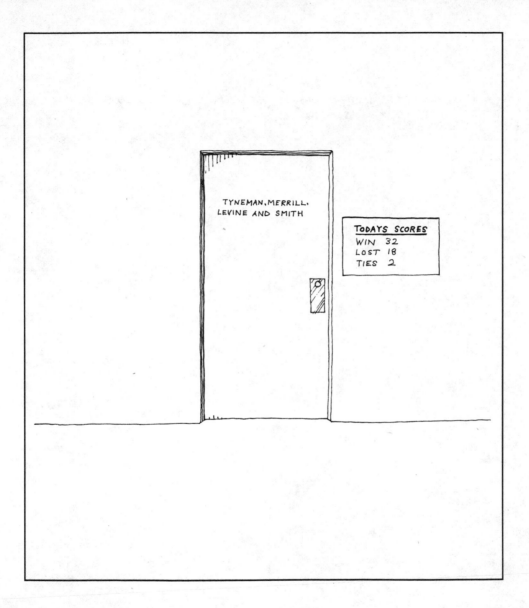

Never... have so many... owed... so much... to so few.

"I think I can get you off with two years, but I'm afraid it's the chair for the hat!"

"And finally after you've read the will, laugh out loud and say I changed my mind and it's all been left to the dog."

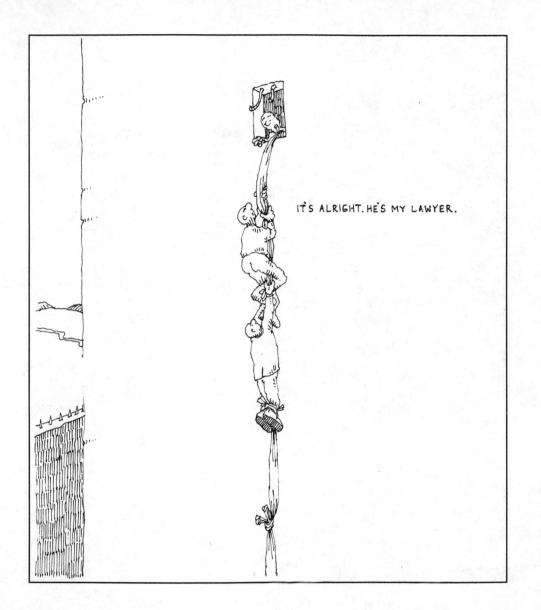

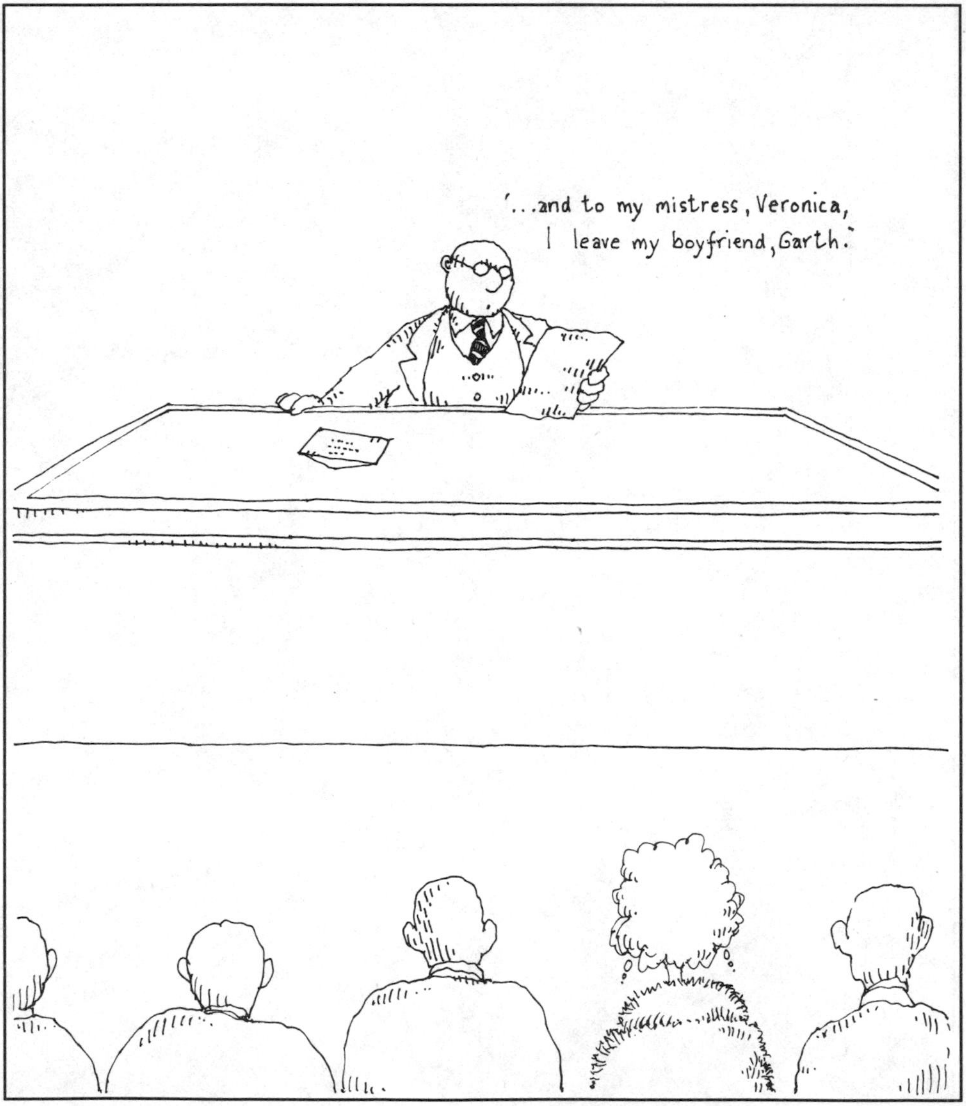
"...and to my mistress, Veronica,
I leave my boyfriend, Garth."

"Even in life he always had his lawyer present."

ELDON E
FURSE III

AND HIS
ATTORNEYS

"And with this ring, nuptial contract, independent inventory and itemized bill . . . I thee wed."

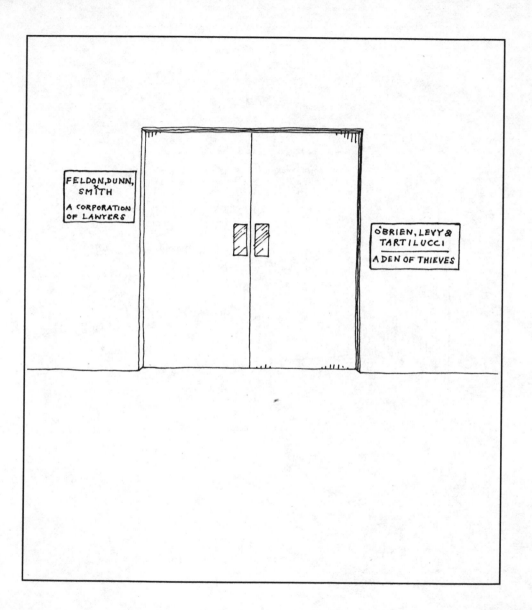

"They're still negotiating for who pays for the beer."

THE LAWYER'S FEE

"And finally for the record, the clerk of the court has odds of 6-4 for guilty, 2-1 not guilty & even for a hung jury."

A LAWYER'S VIEW OF THE WORLD

# About the Author

Simon Bond is a twin, who was born in New York of English parents in 1947. He is not one of life's fit people, mentally or otherwise. Nor is he very tall.

After the usual English education he went to Art School to study graphics, but was asked to leave after his third year for being so damned good looking. A series of jobs followed, including working in the art room of the "Tatler" and managing jewellers.

In 1970 he came back to the U.S., first to New York then to Arizona for his health. Unfortunately, it did not improve his asthma, but he did learn to swear in Yiddish.

During this time he worked various jobs, whilst cartooning at night. Within several years he was published by many of the foremost magazines in America, which included "The Saturday Evening Post" and "Esquire."

In 1981 he resurrected an idea he had first sent to "Esquire" and "National Lampoon" entitled *One Hundred and One Uses of a Dead Cat.* At a dinner party at the home of Terry Jones of "Monty Python" fame he mentioned it and within a short while the English publishers Methuen agreed to publish the book.

Since then it has sold in the region of 1.75 million copies throughout the world, in countries as diverse as Japan and Sweden.

He has published over a dozen books since then and continues to annoy lots of people. And amuse many others.

He now lives with his American wife in a large Jacobean manor in England which they are restoring. And there he continues to follow his interests of antique collecting and idleness in equal amounts.

He also has one dog, two cats and a flock of borrowed sheep. And is surprisingly well mannered and will not embarrass you in expensive restaurants.